D0961589

Home Body

HOME BODY

~~~

John Thorne

Illustrated by Russell Christian

THE ECCO PRESS

THE ECCO PRESS
100 West Broad Street
Hopewell, New Jersey 08525

Published simultaneously in Canada by
Penguin Books Canada Ltd., Ontario

Printed in the United States of America

Library of Congress Cataloging-in-Publication Data

Thorne, John.
    Home body / John Thorne ; illustrated by Russell
Christian — 1st Ecco ed.
        p.   cm.
    ISBN 0-88001-514-4
    I. Title.
  AC8.T485   1996
  081—dc20   96-5280

ISBN 0-88001-514-4

Designed by John Thorne
The text of this book is set in Berling

9 8 7 6 5 4 3 2 1

FIRST EDITION

For Matt

In the smallest theater in the world the
bread crumbs speak.

—Charles Simic,
Dime-Store Alchemy:
The Art of Joseph Cornell

Contents

∾

～

…it isn't a complete building; it has been broken into pieces inside me; a room here, a room there, and then a piece of a hallway that doesn't connect these two rooms, but is preserved as a fragment, by itself. In this way, it is all dispersed inside me—the rooms, the staircases that descend so gracefully and ceremoniously, and other, spiral stairs, where you moved through the darkness as blood moves in the veins…all this is still inside me and will never cease to be there. It is as if the image of this house has fallen into me from an infinite height and shattered upon my ground.

—Rainer Maria Rilke,
The Notebooks of Malte Laurids Brigge

～

And the supreme mystery which Kilman might say she had solved, or Peter might say he had solved, but Clarissa didn't believe either of them had the ghost of an idea of solving, was simply this: here was one room; there another. Did religion solve that, or love?

—Virginia Woolf,
Mrs. Dalloway

The house I built for Gretl is the product of a decidedly sensitive ear and good manners, an expression of great understanding (of a culture, etc.). But primordial life, wild life striving to erupt into the open—that is lacking.

—Ludwig Wittgenstein,
Vermischte Bemerkungen

Home Body

The Keyhole

∾

At the head of the corridor a closed door
led to other corridors, unfurnished
rooms, stairways, and attics. The chill of
unknown things entered through the
door's keyhole.

— Goffredo Parise, *Abecedary*

O N MY WAY FROM HERE TO THERE, young and
broke, I arrange to spend the night with
a friend at his Manhattan apartment. It
is an unusual place for New York, a series of
separate apartment entryways opening onto a
courtyard in which a fountain plays. Three keys
are required for access: one to get into the
courtyard, one for the particular entryway, and
one for the apartment.

My friend is not home. However, perhaps
because I am obviously a college student and
carrying two large, heavy suitcases, someone

lets me into the courtyard, and, then, later, more surprisingly, someone else lets me into the apartment stairwell.

There, on the second floor landing, just outside my friend's door, I spend the night. At one point, the telephone rings incessantly inside the apartment. I learn later that it is my friend himself, calling to explain why he is not there, should I somehow have found a way to slip his lock. Since it is a deadbolt, I have not.

Even though, all through the night, a door on the floor above opens a crack and then immediately shuts, I don't feel like an intruder. Rather, like someone who's stepped out in his bathrobe to get the newspaper and hears the door close and the lock snick shut behind him, I feel the victim of a freakish prank, a silly misunderstanding. This door, when last locked, was not locked against *me*. Again and again, I can't help turning the handle and giving the door a tentative push. Come on, I plead, just let me in.

It astonishes me that we have no special word for this desire to get inside. It is what impels a homeless person to crawl into an empty cardboard box, and to experience, once inside it, as complete a change of atmosphere as if one had stepped out of a snowstorm into a cozy cabin.

In animated cartoons, the doorknob is often transformed into a nose, the keyhole into a mouth. When a door is shut, the passage between outside and in is compressed to a size fit only for an orifice—an ear or eye or mouth.

The keyhole as orifice...this is most plainly true of the keyhole as it once was, a real hole that passed right through the door. When I was a boy, there were keyholes like these in all the doors inside the house. This keyhole allowed the deliciously named skeleton key to be inserted from either side. To ensure both privacy and safety, this key, once one had entered the room with it, could be inserted into the keyhole from the other side, then twisted—so that it could not be shaken or poked out—and left in the lock.

In most houses, however, the skeleton keys were lost in the back of some kitchen drawer and the locks long rusted shut. The keyhole had passed from a functional entity into a metaphor. Anyone familiar with real keyholes knows there is nothing much to be seen through one—certainly nothing to compare to the hold it has over our fantasies.

This, I think, is so because there is, besides the mouth, another bodily orifice with which the keyhole might be associated...one suggested by its shape, its location at exactly groin height, its relationship to the key, and especially its aura of secrecy, the tension between temptation and denial that surrounds any forbidden entry. If a house can be said to have private parts, surely they are these.

I write "parts" because the doorknob must be included, too. With it, this image becomes hermaphroditic and, so, teasingly confused. The key, after all, is little more than an attenuated bone (skeleton keys are called such because all their particularity has been filed away). But the doorknob—which fits so comfortably into the hand and is such a pleasure to hold and gently twist—is the phallus, not as threat, but as familiar.

The door, then, offers something to everyone, not only to the person with the key. Indeed, to unlock, then open, a door is to dispel all mystery, and with it the sense of attraction, even intimacy, radiated by the shut room beyond. But we heighten this instead when—at least in our imagination—we press to the keyhole our eye, to peek; our ear, to listen;

our nose, to smell; our mouth, to whisper through it.

The key is an emblem of power, evidence of the right to enter and so to control. Because of this, for certain people, the key itself is a highly charged erotic toy, and they can't have too many on their key ring. The one thing that interests them about a lock, a room, a body, is to possess its key.

For those without the key or any hope of getting it, there are only two possibilities—which may or may not be offered as a choice—to be locked in or to be locked out. These are two entirely different situations, but they lead to the same state: an endless obsession regarding the holder of the key.

In an ideal world, all doors would have keyholes, but all keys would be lost. In this regard, it might be said that a book is a room whose true interior can only be explored through its keyhole, which is the word. Everything is permitted within, except entry. Unlike a room, a book preserves its mystery forever, because it has no key. ◆

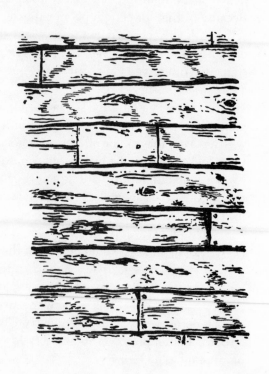

The Floor

❧

BEFORE THERE WERE HOUSES, we humans lived in trees. Or at least we wanted to. I know this because children are enchanted with tree houses, not cave houses; because houses at their best *feel* like trees, being open and sheltering at once; and especially because of the protective fondness we have for trees, as we do for dogs… as if we remember them from a distant time as being not only close but necessary friends.

The tree was the first house, and it is in its image that all succeeding houses have been built. A house tree invites us to climb it, and when we do we find somewhere up the trunk a thick, strong branch to sit on. There, hidden in a room of leafy boughs, we can peer out at the world, as comfortable and safe as we would in a mother's or father's patient, pro-

tecting arms, lifted up and out of the dangerous place below.

Indeed, the phrase "ground floor" contra-
dicts itself—a floor is not the ground. The
space under a tree is only half a shelter;
the ground is hard, cold, and damp. A floor, on
the other hand, should be warm, dry, and re-
silient, somehow possessing *lift*—which is why
there is something almost viscerally distressing
about floors made of concrete.

Nor do floors of pine, oak, or teak call
out for the mitigating softness of carpets, certainly not running wall to wall. The Arabs created such flooring to spread on top of sand. For
them the wood floor, like the tree itself, waits
in paradise.

The wood floor bears the stigmata of its
origin in each of its boards, which are branches
made perfectly flat and straight. Monkeys accommodated themselves to the branch; we
accommodated the branch to ourselves. But
despite their unnatural perfection, boards still
invite children to walk their length, trying not
to tumble off.

We adults always subconsciously note
the width of floorboards when we first enter a
room. Hence the sensation of extravagant

comfort when we encounter one of those old floors made of extrawide boards. The broader the branch, the better our sense of balance. The floor, in short, is where we humans perch.

❧   ❧   ❧

I learn this when I spend a weekend in a summer house by the sea. The house has two floors, the ceiling of the first one nothing more than the floorboards of the second, which are none too tightly joined. In the daytime, the sunshine streaming in through the upstairs windows spills down to us below in broken slats of brightness, as though filtering through leaves.

When night comes, I am the last one up to bed. As I sit by the fireplace, smoking the evening's final, luxurious cigarette, I hear the muffled thud of a shifting body and remember the children asleep upstairs, spread out on quilts laid down on the floor.

I imagine one of them waking for a moment, smelling the soothing, mingled odor of wood fire and tobacco smoke rising between the floorboards, seeing faint lines of firelight flickering just above her on the sloping roof.

Rolling over and peeking down through

the crack beside her head, she sees me hunched over the dying embers and feels safe and hidden, among her own little tribe of monkeys high up in the tree.

The house comes to me then all of a piece: chimney as trunk, shingles as leaves, and beams and boards as an intertwining lattice of branches and boughs. On these I see sprawled the tangle of young, sleeping bodies, suspended just above my head. It is a physically warm, impersonally sensual imagining, the intimacy of a burrow without the claustral fug.

Although this image is light and airy, the bodily sensation it evokes is heavy and full. As I lie down beside the fire and roll up in my sleeping bag, I've already fallen asleep. ◆

The Bed

∾

My bed is my brother.

— *Swahili saying*

JUST TURNED TWENTY, I drop out of college and move into a tenement on Manhattan's Lower East Side. Free furniture in that neighborhood is hard to come by, so I sleep each night on a straw mat rolled out on the floor. My body does not, at first, like this, not knowing how to settle into comfort when none is given (though any dog could show it how).

Once the knack is learned, however, I find that, down there in the dark, the fall into sleep is precipitous...and entirely different from going to sleep in bed. In fact, it is the closest an adult can come to a baby's sleep—

though not the way that experience is usually imagined.

Sprawled out on the floor, I, too, become exposed and helpless. The smallest pieces of furniture tower above me. Although the floor vibrates to the house's every creak and groan, my mind, rather than give alarm, retreats even deeper into sleep, and each such noise is absorbed as another lurch in my roller-coaster dreams.

Still, to sleep on the floor does mean I can't fall out of bed. This fact always freshly astonishes me. Awake, I sometimes roll off the mat intentionally, just to experience again this vivid feeling of *not* falling, of floating on the floor.

However, this corporeal lightness thickens my sleep still further, for nothing inside me now remains alert. I often wake tangled in bed linen, spilled out onto the floor. Unable to fall from bed, I fall instead into a slumber without bottom, deep as dying.

No surprise that, returning to a normal bed, I begin to regularly fall out of it. My body, grown accustomed to its magical buoyancy, continues to plummet sleepward—only to find that once deep place now full of shoals.

The shallows beneath the bed drag hard at my dreams. I find myself flying mere inches from the ground and at such terrifying speeds that I wake up drenched with sweat....

Unhorsed. Beds are harder than horses to fall from—but we ride them, even so, and I have to learn to ride mine again. In dreams begin responsibilities: floor sleep like crib sleep has something incontinent in its nature. It is the frailty we had to overcome to win our first bed, with its short but precarious distance from the floor.

A mattress on a floor is only a pad; lifted up and set on legs it becomes a body: taut, muscular, supple. Its furniture-like solidity is illusory. We learned to ride it so long ago we forget we ever did, but our bed remains the same stolid, gentle steed that we once tamed to take us down to sleep.

Each night we climbed under its clothing and pressed ourself against its skin. At first, feeling wobbly on our perch, we clung to its broad, strong back. But it proved no hard task, after all, to find our balance there—much easier, in fact, than the one we had yet to gain on our own two unstable feet.

Lifted from the floor, a bed becomes

more than a place to sleep: the continuous subtle alertness needed to stay aloft there makes us conscious, not only of its body, but of our own. At first, as children, tucked snugly under sheet and blanket, we want only the safety of that tight embrace. But then we gradually begin, in the secrecy of darkness, to shake it loose…and, inch by inch, to slowly, innocently, slide our body through the soft, resisting sheets.

We do this because the bed's baggy clothing is so accommodating to inquisitive limbs—and because mastery has made the bed our own. The space beneath the covers is ours even before our room is—just as our bed will become the last place we surrender when age or illness creeps up to box us in.

Safe in bed. Yes, but only because of the risk of falling out. This is why, though logic might suggest a bed have the sides of a bathtub to keep a sleeper safe, the image conjures up only cribs and coffins—with nothing, out-of-hospital, in between. Somewhere within us we still remember: because of those sides our crib filled up with sleep and, helpless and unknowing, we all but drowned there every night. ◆

The Closet

⚮

A HOUSE LIVES IN THE SPACE where we do not. Every house must have its own space, a place in which to find its meaning apart from us. This is not exactly a secret place, but it is *its* place, separate and equal to our own. The cellar is its base, the attic the apex, and every closet a column: a temple of invisible, unlived-in space.

We walk among the pillars of this temple without ever noticing their existence, but their enigmatic shadows are registered in some primal corner of our mind. It is these that give a house its sense of depth, of mystery, of being large enough not only to contain our bodies but our selves.

Today, though the attic has shrunk into a crawl space and the cellar into the empty box that is a basement, the pillars remain intact, rising like obelisks out of an ancient ruin, faded reminders of a time when houses also had souls. The closet, when deep and dark enough, can contain within itself both cellar and attic, all at once the dark below and the light above—and the secret column that connects them still.

When I was a child, we moved into a house that had a closet with a tiny wooden door set into its back wall. I was filled with sudden wonder and the certainty that I had been admitted into a conspiracy all houses have against those who live in them...holding back the very last room of all.

Just to see that tiny door was to know how much I longed to live in a place that had its secrets, whose center was still a mystery. But houses are no longer built with doors not meant to be opened, and behind that tiny door was nothing but the interior of a fuse box. To-day, all doors are accounted for; closets keep their mysteries only because they are rooms whose doors we ourselves insist must always be kept closed.

Closets make us uneasy. We cannot dominate them the way we do other rooms. We feel like intruders when we go into them, strangers even. The closet is the room's room, the place where it retreats from us when we have filled it too much with ourselves. We may go into closets, but we do not belong in them: even the things we stash there fall away from us to take on their own poor selves again.

Go into the bedroom closet and clear a space to sit down on the floor. Feel how the clothes that hang there press hard against you, unwilling to give you room. They may accommodate your body when you wear them, but among their own kind they pretend not to know you at all. Here is where they come to shake your smell out of their fibers and, squeezing flat against their neighbors, to obliterate all memory of your form.

Up at the ceiling, cobwebs float on the breath of this clothing, on the sighs of the shoes. You can smell these exhalations as they rise past you, half human and half not, a disquieting commingling of the acrid and the sweet. These things are our possessions, but in this place, bleak as a servant's room, each of them reveals remnants of a private self that a life of service has all but scoured out.

In some deep part of ourselves, we understand that our possessions struggle against this usage all the time. The closet is less storage area than a place where both sides find respite. So, just as it is easy enough to bury things in the mind but not to unearth them later, things get put into closets that choose never to come back out. What is hidden resists being found, and we sometimes buy a thing anew rather than face the oblique tenacity of what has been put away.

For this reason, we can never be sure what our closets actually contain. Should we decide to clean one out, there are often objects buried too deeply in it to be found…even though they are sitting right before our eyes. These are the things that, when we move into a house or apartment, wait for us on closet shelves. Each one is completely ordinary, and yet we turn it over and over in our hands…an empty bottle that, having floated into our lives, now obstinately refuses to disgorge its message.

Closets serve us best when we decide not to look into them too closely, which is why people who keep theirs too neatly end up having no closets at all. Better instead to find the house with one more closet than we will ever need, for that is the house that can make us feel truly at home. ◆

The Chest of Drawers

❧

It is a profound truth that a well-ordered
drawer is a dangerous thing.

— *after Gershom Scholem*

THE BUREAU IT IS ALSO CALLED, after a
French writing table with drawers: a
little office all by itself, it was, once
upon a time when a drawer could hold all you
needed to run one. We might also call it a
dresser—or chiffonier—except that those
have mirrors and ours does not. It is just a box:
a box with drawers.

No, more than a box, a chest. Chests are
distinguished from boxes by the fact that we
have chests, too. And a chest of drawers *is* almost like a human chest. Even as children we
notice the certain correspondence between
our own dinkweed frame and a chest of drawers—the upright posture, the double knobs.

Of course, when our two knobs are tugged on, no drawer pulls open. But imagine if one did: the same familiar mess…and mother making us straighten it double-quick. Heart here, liver there, kidneys set out side by side. A tidy drawer is like an anatomy chart—a place for everything, everything in its place.

Not so inside us, really…nor in our drawers, either, except as constant struggle resists the tide. This is the universal law: behind the benign, clean-scrubbed fronting of the chest of drawers, the contents move towards mess.

How could it be otherwise? Our public face says that we put things away in them; our true self knows we hide things there instead. Our drawers hold what touches our body. To touch these things is, by extension, to touch ourselves. There is no name for what we put away and close the drawer on: it is, by very essence, private.

Although some drawers have things actually hidden in them, most do not. Their aura of concealment comes from what they protect within. The bedroom is already a private place; each drawer condenses and thus intensifies that privacy into the most intimate possible space.

This is why the drawers that entice us most are shallow but commodious—to pull such a drawer out slowly, revealing everything inside it bit by bit, is like drawing scandals from a gossip. No chest ever has enough.

Consequently, drawers ascend in order of increasing intimacy. The largest drawer, at the very bottom, is little more than an ordinary chest. Into it we stuff the things that are our most public declaration of self: sweaters, sweatshirts, forgotten summer wear, and—if we wear them only in other people's houses—our one pair of pajamas.

The topmost drawer, on the contrary, where our own body hides our heart and hence our feelings, is the drawer best shaped to hold our letters, items of personal value, photographs, sex toys…and, of course, small clothes.

Underpants are called drawers, too: perhaps because they once were tied with a draw string, or because we draw them up our legs to put them on. To get into someone's drawers…the connection is gratuitous, accidental, and yet the confusion gives us pleasure. It alerts us to the erotics of the drawer.

Or, to put it another way, the erotics of

order. I think of the drawer in which everything is perfectly folded, each pile primly sorted and neatly laid on lavender paper—the drawer of someone who, even in their most private chamber, keeps desire hidden still. Hidden, yet visible—for such drawers have a concupiscence all their own.

If you disagree, ask what you would most delight in finding, given the chance to look into the drawers of someone you desire: neatness, or mess? Something almost electric happens when one lets one's fingers touch such secret neatness....

The erotics of order. When we shut our intimate clothes away in drawers, they are hidden, not only from the eyes of others, but also from our own. The drawer is a dark place, yes—and what reason do we have to think things *sleep* there...or, if they do, to be sure of what they dream?

Rather than contemplate such questions, we struggle to keep our drawers in order, ever disentangling the contents of their promiscuous embrace. Only a mind strong enough to carelessly display its depths allows its drawers to remain in a wanton state. To the rest of us it just seems to happen. Thus that sobering moment when, on a Sunday morning, we pull one open and are embarrassed to find there, framed in shameless dishabille, the face of Saturday night. ◆

The Stairs

⌇

MY GRANDPARENTS LIVED on the first floor of a large, two-family house, renting the floor above. Long before I came along, my grandfather, tiring of the squabbling and scurrying of children overhead, converted the second floor into two one-bedroom apartments. From then on, the tenants were all single.

However, to put a new hallway through to one of the bedrooms, he had to remove the bottom third of the attic stairs. These then ran straight into a wall, four feet above the landing. There, to give access to them, a section of the railing had been sawn away. An agile child of twelve could grab hold of one of the now wobbly banisters and leg himself up onto the bottom step.

I get up on these attic steps every time we come to visit. That is the easy part...I con-

veniently forget the terror of getting back down. Then, my leg, stretched full length, flails in vain for contact with the banister, until my nerve flees and I scream for help.

The very thought of it makes my grandmother's heart leap up her throat; this is the one climb forbidden me in a house that is a treat of stairs. The basement flight, for example, plunges steeply into darkness from the bottom of a broom closet. The front stairwell, inspired by a long-ago stay in New Mexico, has whitewashed walls, hewn oak doorways, steps covered with terra-cotta-colored stucco, and a wrought-iron banister and chandelier. The back stairs alone are completely ordinary— but they lead up to that missing attic turn.

Like Bluebeard's wife, I want access only to the forbidden place. I believe that the attic is my goal, with its steamer trunks in eternal storage, the piles of old *Life* magazines with pictures of the action and carnage of World War II, which can engross me for hours at a time. But the truth is that I have come up the stairs just to sit at the top of them and stare back down that dizzying slope to where they end, smack into a wall.

Escalators, I am discovering, aren't the

only stairs in motion. All stairs have steps, and steps mean movement: hence, a *flight* of stairs, a stair*way*. At first, elevation might seem sufficient explanation for their urgency. After all, climbing them, the body does feel heavier and heavier, as if being primed by gravity for its later hurtling descent.

Still, a stairway isn't merely a means of getting up and down. It's also a kind of doorway between floors, which is to say, between two competing realms of space. These each exert their force. Once on the first step of a staircase, you've left the place it exits from, no matter that you still remain in view.

Even as the upstairs reaches down to grasp you, the downstairs is unwilling to let you go. Both claim this space…but somewhere in its middle lies a point of equilibrium, where we often instinctively pause to regain our own. Its existence is why stairs are so tranquil to sit on, the trick being to find the fulcrum, the still place. Children have no hesitation sliding up and down the steps until they hit it—here…no, here…no, *here*.

A hallway, also, is between here and there. But when you sit down in one it becomes a room—or worse, an *ante*room. Hallways are where attendants and applicants wait and where children who are being punished are made to sit. It's no punishment to sit on a flight of stairs.

Doorway, stairway—both frame the border between those countries we call rooms. But in the one that space is compressed into almost nothing; in the other it has been stretched apart. It's like two views of the same accordion, first closed, then pulled open... slantwise, so that we might keep our footing as we hurry across the pleats. ◆

The Window

∾

A SHORT ROW ACROSS the channel from our family cottage on the coast of Maine is a deserted island, once the site of a summer colony. By the time I begin to explore the place, the houses are barely more than tottering hulks, ruthlessly scavenged of all that nearby islanders found useful, the floors ripped up for boards and the chimneys toppled for brick.

A single house survives this massacre, a small, square, two-story Victorian cottage standing in full view above the beach. Perhaps because of this public location, vandals, although they had scoured it clean—doors and windows included—have let the building be.

The second floor is made up entirely of three roomy bedrooms tucked under a mansard roof. These, especially, though damaged, seem unviolated. Bleached wallpaper still clings to plaster walls, the floorboards hold firm, the slate roof repels the rain. All that is required to take up tenancy—at least for the month of August—is a broom.

I don't need even that, having come only to sit and eat my lunch and look over the shimmering bay at the dark green line of coast beyond. Because these windows have been stolen entire, the floor is not littered with shards of glass, and what the room lacks in amenities, it makes up for in intensity of space.

The windows in this house had been made six feet high, with sills set a mere two feet above the floor. Without glass or sash, they fill the room with air and light—take the view and set it in my lap.

A small branch from a tree outside has reached through the south window to the sunlight pouring through the west one and has burst out into leaf. Each time I come up and see it, bright and green as in a fairy tale, I feel a tug of incredulous delight.

If the actual windows were there, gap-toothed, broken, the room, for all its charm, would still be a ruin. But these simple oak-framed openings seem chosen, and imagination accepts the room as habitation, its vulnerability a point of charm—no bed in summer is the worse roofed with a leafy canopy.

Instead, the sense of being inside becomes all that much more palpable, a shirt tossed over the shoulders and worn by grace of friction, cloth against skin. This room has that same weightlessness, as if the outdoors needs only to give one deep breath to draw all its contents out. Standing in front of one of these shin-high sills, my feet begin to lose their purchase on the floor. It is my body rather than my brain that felt light-headed, as if solidity itself were leaching out the frame.

Unlike swimming underwater, where reality and sensation merge, before an open window stability feels like a useless, even foolish, burden. It is this sensation, not any fear of falling, that makes me step back and close my eyes until my body regains its feeling of not only accustomed but necessary weight.

A window allows us to turn the inside out and let the outside in. It is a rupture point between two separate realities, less a passageway than a hole. To truly see out of one you must also be able to fall out of it; otherwise, no matter how much you look, you still won't know exactly where you are.

Space and light, openness and closedness, are experienced most immediately by our eyes, but their truth is finally tactile—they need to be felt to be made real. Glass is visually transparent but sensually opaque; it alone is not enough to make a window. What can't be opened is only another kind of wall.

A French window is the most sensual of such openings, for it is wall, door, and window, all at once. The epithet conveys the general suspicion of such licentious access—and, even with that disclaimer, it still unnerves: the general preference is to call it, instead, a door.

A glass door, at least, can be understood. A window that offers such intimacy is abhorrent to the current puritanism which conspicuously designs windows to limit access: triple-paned, tinted, and sometimes even hermetically sealed. Better, I think, to make do with blinds, shutters, shades…window garments that casually fall open or get zipped up tight, depending on the season and the company.

The curtains are set aflutter by a sudden breeze, the cool, moist harbinger of an approaching storm. Some jump at the touch and hurry through the house, slamming windows shut. If, instead, it entices you to go fling the nearest one wide open, you, too, know that there are times when a window, like a piece of clothing, is most appealing when easiest to push aside. ◆

The Electric Light

∾

YOUNG AND ALONE IN NEW YORK CITY, I
go out walking on summer evenings.
Sometimes I wander through the West
Village, sometimes along the crosstown streets
that pass from Gramercy Park to Chelsea. I
walk there because these streets are safe, because the glare of the arc lamps filtering
through the leaves of the plane trees transforms the sidewalks into underwater passages
of light and shadow, but also and mostly because I am a voyeur.

These are streets lined with brown-
stones, private residences into whose ground-
and first-floor windows I can furtively stare. I
have no interest in the people who live there
nor—at least in any covetous sense—in their
possessions. If a room is inhabited by its owners, I quickly move on. I linger only when I pass
an illuminated, empty room that seems—for a

few illicit, dizzyingly exciting seconds—to invite me in.

What draws me to these windows as a moth to a flame is the seductive intimacy of the incandescent electric bulb. Because we are so used to it, we forget how powerful it really is. The windows of a house lit by candles do not glow until the sun has completely set. Even then, what one sees from outside a candlelit house is an inner darkness punctuated with tiny points of light. But an electric bulb floods a room with an illumination so bright that instead of the reflectors and mirrors once necessary for amplifying indoor light, we now employ shades, dimmers, and low-wattage filaments to *diminish* it.

A wealth of light—this not only distinguishes the modern house from all others but is the essential element of its charm. We illuminate the kitchen, the bathroom, the garage, or any room that is fundamentally a place of work with wall sconces or ceiling fixtures, and often with the cool, heatless, neutral glow of the fluorescent tube, which provides a simulacrum of daylight, of perpetual noon.

However, in the rooms in which we live out the drama of our lives—especially the living room and the bedroom—we use incandescent bulbs. This is partly because these have a filament that hotly burns, and their warmth, and the comfort of that warmth, fills a room with life. But these lights, always set around the room below eye level, keep it in perpetual twilight, that moment of the day when the whole world recedes into intimacy and what is most personal becomes most important.

Candlelight, which we think of as romantic, is so only because its feeble illumination heightens our other senses, making the presence of a loved one more palpable. No matter how many candles glitter in the candelabra, darkness still comes to hover in the corners. It is an essentially helpless light, and thus the appropriate illumination for a church, where each taper is a metaphor for a human soul: weak, flickering, easily snuffed out...and surrounded by an unplumbable immensity of dark.

In a room lit by electric light, however, any shadow is an intentional effect, and so without authentic mystery. What electric light offers us is theater, and it consequently encourages us to see our lives not as spiritual but as theatrical events.

The theater of the home. In a culture wealthy enough for every citizen to own a private playhouse, the play itself can be dispensed with; the actors play themselves. And the warmth, the brightness of the electric light licks them with attention. It provides the anticipation of an audience without the chilling reality of having to keep a real one entertained.

A well-placed lamp is all that's needed to bring a scene to life. In even the shabbiest of sets, it catches the luster of the tabletop, picks out the colors in the carpet. The tattiness, the dustiness of the furnishings recede. When I lived alone, I would go through the house at night and turn on all the lamps, so that as I went from room to room I would always feel *expected*.

From each of these lamps there falls a shaft of light. These illuminate a part of the sofa, the upper corner of the bed, a heap of papers spilled across a desk. This light is directed not at these pieces of furniture but at the space before them, the place where the drama will take place.

Drama, before anything else, is expectation. It is this sense of longing, which can be felt as a palpable desire, that draws me to stare into those windows. In certain rooms, at certain moments, the sight of a certain kind of emptiness can be as disturbingly desirable as a glimpse of a naked human body.

What is a voyeur, after all, if not an audience of one? This illuminated space is the arena of the actor, and hence of the exhibitionist. What is it that I expect to do in these rooms if I ever lose all self-control and climb through one of these windows? The answer can only be that, on this new, strange, seductively appealing stage set, I think I will better put on the performance that is myself.

The scene: going to bed. Enter stage right; sit at the edge of the bed; sigh; stretch; kick the slippers off; lift up your legs and slide between the sheets; pull up the covers; and now—end of scene—switch off the light. Audience and actor may be one and the burst of applause implicit. Even so, the lights in the windows of each house on the street all proclaim the announcement: show tonight. ◆

The Kitchen Sink

❧

MY PARENTS BUY AN OLD MAINE farm house and discover that its only indoor convenience is a kitchen sink. It has a hand pump to supply washing water (tiny, undulating organisms swim about in this, reducing its appeal as a source of drink) and a drain that releases its contents directly out into the yard.

They make do with this arrangement—and bottled drinking water—for some time, while a well is drilled, a septic tank interred, and the plumbing installed. They shower at a nearby campground and use the local laundromat, learning what—by chance—I myself am also just discovering: that cleanliness starts, not with the body or the clothes, but with the dishes…or, rather, with the kitchen sink.

This is because I, too, am living without one. My apartment is cobbled together out of two former bedrooms, both with working fire-places, floor-to-ceiling windows, and ornate moldings. However, the kitchen has been jerry-built onto a tiny outdoor balcony. Walled in, it becomes tinier still: room enough just for a table, a refrigerator, and a stove.

There is a bathroom, too, of course, but its sink is much too small for washing anything but silverware. This leaves the dishes, pots, and glasses to the enormous marble tub. It is rumored that the dishes wait until I take a bath myself, which isn't true. I wash them the hard way, kneeling on the floor and cursing.

This arrangement allows me, unlike my parents, to keep up a pretense of civilized existence—I entertain lavishly out of that midget kitchen—but guests still feel its essential seediness as a perpetual, subliminal itch. That rumor is half joke, half fear.

To wash something is to bring it back to itself. The washed plate and the washed hand are two different kinds of freshness. Our hands get clean washing the dishes, but we rinse them afterwards, anyway; the dishes' cleanliness isn't theirs.

A hand washed clean of dishwashing: this is a paradox only in terms of sanitation.

Restoration of order—the plate cleaned of food, the hand cleaned of cleaning—is the purpose of most ablutions, which is why as children we soon grasp that the gesture is more important than the act.

Emphasis, then, is everything—and here, especially, indoor plumbing has come into its own. The rush of water from the tap permits not only washing up, but actual washing away. This is the difference between the tub and the shower, and the old-fashioned wash basin and the modern sink.

However, this also means that the sink is both a place where clean water can collect and a place out of which dirty water goes. No matter that the sink may be scrubbed to a sanitary gloss, the hole in its center leads to a place that, by definition, cannot be cleaned. Sinks have drains, and—as all roads lead to Rome—all drains lead to the same primordial midden.

Put a sink in any place outside the kitchen or the bathroom, and you risk summoning up the ambiance of the cheap hotel. A sink not in its right place is necessarily suspect, not because of the uses it might be put to, but because of our fear of what might come back up.

Even too disorderly a rush of refuse *down* a drain unnerves us, like a mob of children all let out of school at once. We establish orderly departures by giving each sink its special purpose, its particular brand of sludge. What goes down the kitchen sink should keep out of the bathroom one, and vice versa—no spitting toothpaste down the kitchen drain… nor washing dishes in the tub.

Which one is worse? Consider: most of us in one mood can eat lunch off our own unwashed breakfast plate, while in another, won't take even a bite off someone else's fork. Unwatched, undisciplined, the self leaves handprints everywhere, which is why the solitary life is by nature solipsistic, or—more bluntly put—unkempt.

The bachelor remembers to wash only at the point of suffocation…or at the arrival of a guest. Hearing the knock on the door, he (or she) heads straight into the kitchen. Company is much more likely to note the condition of the cup in which they get their coffee than that of the outstretched, welcoming, not-quite-sanitary hand. ◆

The Fireplace

∽

IN HOUSES WHERE IT SERVES a true purpose, the fireplace is large and solid, an inescapable presence that gives a home its own true north. Winter or summer, to whatever distant room one wanders, an inner compass immediately orients itself toward the safe, the protecting place. Just the way the heart—although it is not in the exact center of the body—is our body's center, so is the fireplace the center of the home.

A fireplace is, first of all, the fire's *place*. The fire lives there and, in living, fills the house with an aura of habitation, the ambience and warmth that is the feeling of "inside." However, even as the fire feeds the house, it also hungers for it. Let loose, it would devour everything, leaving standing—in the middle of its devastation—the chimney and fireplace alone.

Modern means of heating, for all their safety and convenience, lack this reciprocal attending, the basis of the unique intimacy that has always existed between a house and its fireplace. Whether built in the middle of such a building—as with the classic saltbox or Cape Cod—or up one side of it—as with the Rhode Island "stone-ender"—the fireplace is, in fact, a *massif central* that stores up the heat upon which the rooms will continue to nurse, even after the fire itself has long burnt out.

Thus, wherever it is put, such a fireplace draws every room toward it and, by doing so, pulls them together into a home. When the day grows dark or cold, the house turns inward around its fireplace and puts its back to the bleak outside…deepening the sense of shelter for those who live there, for the very walls exude safety and warmth.

I come, one late November, to spend a weekend at the family's Maine summer cottage, which is built around such a compacted heart of mortar and stone. I arrive just as the sun is setting, and the first thing I do is carry in several armloads of firewood and build a fire.

But, for a long time afterwards, there is no comfort in it.

I wrap blankets around myself and pull the rocker right up to the blaze. Even though my face, my hands, my shins are so hot that they hurt, the rest of me is freezing. The cold lies like a rug on the floor, chilling my feet right through my shoes.

Meanwhile, night comes, and the wind, blowing off the ocean, pushes tiny flakes of frozen brine through every crevice in the walls. I can feel it even through the blankets. I begin to think with dread of that block of ice that is the bed. The thought comes to me that a person might freeze to death in front of a roaring fire.

But then the studs and joists begin, ever so slowly, to ease themselves. The pores in the floor open and exhale a sweet scent of polish and wood. The stone mass has begun to radiate its soft but penetrating heat right into the structure of the house.

There is no hurrying this process; more wood on the fire just sends more heat straight up the chimney. But once the warmth is there, it stays. At bedtime, the fire can be banked and left to settle into sleep. In the morning, there are only a few embers smoldering under the ashes, but the stone hearth still warms the hands.

This residual heat embodies a paradox in our relationship with the fireplace. Unlike oil heat, which is either on or off, fireplace heat is always both on *and* off. Long after the fire dies away, its warmth lingers like a memory in the stone mass.

But, as it burns, the fire is also constantly slipping away up the chimney—the way out of the house that we do not usually think of as an exit, although it is the only doorway that is always open.

This transience is one of the forces that animates our reveries as we sit before the fire, for we bask not only in its warmth but also in intimations of our own mortality. On a winter's night, the cold pressing in from everywhere, the restlessness of the flames never lets us forget that every fire must sometime go out for good. When it does, even before the place that holds it has a chance to cool, inside will already be slipping up the chimney… and outside will be preparing to come completely in. ◆

The Attic

◆

I AM SIXTEEN. My family is living for the moment in what could almost pass for a mansion, on an army post designed by the architect Stanford White. This house, the post commander's residence, is a huge brick pile, with a separate servant stairway, a butler's pantry, a drawing room with sliding glass-paned doors and oak parquet floors. The attic is a warren of servants' quarters, tiny rooms that at one time had housed a butler, a cook, and several maids, now empty of furniture, habitation, life.

I am fascinated by this place, lingering here for hours, not up to any mischief, just a lonely teenager haunting desolated human space. Any empty house is all attic, but only derelict, once-lived-in houses possess that mix of unease and melancholy that calls up thoughts of spirits. In these places, however, it is we who are the ghosts.

This attic is redolent of such abandonment and, in daylight at least (I never dare go up at night), is balm to my adolescent sense of being at once outcast and above it all. Here I can go to escape my family but still remain at home, in a place full of mysterious silences, glorious light, and a view that reaches for miles.

Few attics offer the forlorn complexity of a deserted servants' hall, but there is a simpler sadness, a sense of want and waste, to those which have never been inhabited at all, with their unfinished floorboards, dust- and fly-encrusted windows, and studs delimiting walls that are never to be built. This is because for most adults the attic is only barely to be considered habitable space.

Like the front door, the attic provides a borderland between inside the house and out. The entryway insulates against the street, the attic against the elements. Indigents, not householders, sleep in doorways; the attic is a home for owls and bats. Too hot in summer, too cold in winter, dripping water every time it rains…to inhabit the garret or attic apartment—although Samuel Johnson wrote an essay on the pleasures of living in one—is to slum.

The garret, my dictionary tells me (speaking itself in an unexpectedly Johnsonian tone), is "an attic, usually a small, wretched one." This seems unjust: garret rooms are by definition cramped, since they are usually shoved in beneath a sloping roof. In fact, the less pinched the room, the less it is a garret—a bedroom tucked in the attic of a single-story bungalow has more romance and sense of height than the apartments on the top floor of a six-story apartment house.

The word "garret" comes from the Old French, where it meant a watchtower and, by contraction, that tiny room at the top where the watching took place. If the house itself is already two stories tall, the attic windows open onto a world very different from the one seen from other floors. As high as the treetops, or even higher, it pokes its head above the realm of the household, out of the comfortable closure of the neighborhood and into a starker, more lonely world of distance and height.

Those who don't live in them think of

attic rooms as inconvenient—all those stairs!
—and dangerous in case of fire, but at least
dreamy and quiet, close to bird calls and far
from traffic. Here, certainly, they are wrong. If
attics were truly sleep-conducive, peaceful
places, the choicest bedrooms would be put
there, and they're not.

For the bedroom to feel intimate, it has
to be both apart from and a part of daily life,
just that one level up. Take the extra flight of
stairs into the attic, and the silence that greets
you is the expression of another kind of close-
ness—that of the night outside, waiting to play
havoc with your dreams.

Apartment buildings deal with this the
way that ocean liners do—by orienting us to a
different idea of space. In them, where we are
has to do with the corridor, the elevator, the
entrance hall—in other words, the trail that
will lead us back out of the maze. Apartment
towers only regain their spacial truth when the
power fails and the elevators refuse to run.
Then those tiny rooms, twenty or thirty stories
up, start to compress. That amazing view sucks
the air right out the windows, and the inhabi-
tants suddenly realize where they are. ◆

The Bathtub

༄

A FRIEND AND I ARE FLOATING in his sailboat down the Bagaduce, a tidal river off Penobscot Bay. A light breeze has brought us up on the last of the flood, and now, sails idly flapping, we coast back on the ebb. I sit in the cockpit, legs propped up on the seat opposite, basking in the afternoon sun. I think, "This is just like being in a bathtub, except the water is on the outside."

A pleasant confusion. A bathtub *is* surprisingly like a sailboat. It is voluptuously (if also somewhat tamely) boat-shaped. Water splashes softly against its sides. When you're lying in one, the shower curtain becomes very much a sail. It is tricky work getting in and out of either, and both require short moments of strenuous reaching around…followed by much longer spells of lazing about.

But the most important thing they share

is their sense of buoyancy. As a child, I needed no prior sailboat ride to imagine my bathtub floating down the street. All that was required was being afloat. What did it matter, after all, if it was the tub that was bobbing on the waves, or me? What I wanted was that balmy sense of being lifted up, the promise in the tidal rush of the water down the drain that I too might be swept away.

Perhaps because I fell out of beds but not out of tubs, the bathtub always seemed an especially safe and comforting place. I hated the fact that, unlike my bed, the tub was situated in a place where one faced the threat of interruption. What I wanted—had I ever dared to imagine such a thing—was a *bath*-room: a room with nothing in it but a bath.

I know this now, having seen a photograph, taken in an English house, of a bathtub that has been given a room of its own. It is admirable enough to deserve this, being enormously accommodating and raised up off the floor on four massive leonine feet.

There it stands, squarely in the middle of what looks like a bedroom, except that *it* is the bed. A small cabinet and a comfortable-looking easy chair are all that keep it company... no sink, no toilet, no shower. Furthermore, it rests on a floor of polished wood.

To be sure, this was a high-sided tub, and there were plenty of thick Turkish towels stacked on the cabinet, to stand on as well as in. But what that shining floor proclaims is—this is a *bath*room; this is a bathtub meant for the long…unhurried…soak.

The room in that picture is suffused with light. Two large windows, curtained at the sides, rise from floor to ceiling on the outside wall. Sunlight streams in. There is none of the murky secrecy of pulled shades or pebbled glass. One can lie in this tub and look right outside. An afternoon bath—the thought of it makes me dizzy.

Lovemaking may be best before ablutions, but simple love—for me—is most palpable during them. Unlike the uncomplicated familiarity of, say, the college shower room—where roommate, friends, myself stand each beneath our separate spigot, hair unsculpted, faces scrubbed of masks and bodies of postures, unsexed as children and fraternal as brothers—a single bathtub in a room makes it into an intimate and much more erotic place.

Think of the tub as a large mouth, the

silky, steaming water its cleansing tongue. Like a cat cleaning its kittens, or a bitch its pups, our bathing cleans us less of dirt than of estrangement, licking at us gently until we smell of nothing but body and bath.

I imagine the woman I live with coming in from her usual walk and saying, "I'm so hot. Let's go upstairs and have a soak." We go up to that room and fill the tub with sweet-smelling water. She disrobes and slips in. I sink into the easy chair beside her, lazily stirring the water with my hand, and watch her turn the taps to stem the flow of tepid water, then take up her sponge, unself-consciously absorbed in the familiar, soothing ritual.

The window is wide open. Warm air floats in, carrying the smell of sunlight, the distant mutter of the day. Time slides by, slowly enough for us to feel its passing. And there is no nonsense about getting clean. ◆

The Chair

∾

I AM HAVING A HARD TIME SLEEPING. Tired of tossing and turning on my narrow share of bed, I leave my companion to her dreams, take my pillow and a blanket, go into the living room, and spread out on the rug. I do fall asleep, but sometime a little after dawn I wake up again and lie there drowsily, the furniture lumbering above me in the half light. From down beneath they seem less like artifacts than like a herd of domestic animals, some breed of fabulous mooncalf, asleep in their strange corral.

Right beside me stands a chair. I look up into its pathetic underbelly and think, what a strange simulacrum of a beast. Its body is grotesquely inverted to mirror ours. Children may sit in laps, but adults, except when amorous, do not. We don't sit on a chair's lap but on its seat; nor do we lean against its chest but against its back. If chairs had faces, those, too, would be turned away, eyes to the wall.

Think of a bear or tiger skin rug, with head attached. These things are never made to lie belly up, legs spread out as submissive as a cub's, face staring back at us in utter bafflement at this humiliating turn of events. No, apparently even for great white hunters, perpetual abject surrender gets on the nerves. So, the beast gets flipped over and, allowed to remain oblivious to its fate, keeps something of its ferocious dignity.

Of course, a chair has no former fierceness to temper its current humbled state. To the extent that chairs take after any animal, they most resemble dogs. Dogs, as such, don't exist in nature, nor, unlike, say, horses, do they do well when returned there.

Dogs have been formed by human desire. They come in many shapes and sizes, not one of them planned or even wanted by the dogs themselves. Dogs, like chairs, wish only to please.

Also, as dogs can be classified as either work dog or pet, chairs can be similarly divided into the hard and the soft. The hard chair in its ideal form is not so much uncomfortable as energizing. We sit in one to do something: eat a meal, watch a movie, write a letter, ride a subway or a bus.

Hard chairs are socializing instruments, encouraging movement and so facilitating talk. The softer the chair, the more effort it takes to drag our attention, as our bodies, out of it. This is why living room furniture often looks softer than it really is. It welcomes the guest but is equally ready to propel him on his way. The truly comfy chairs are hidden in the den.

These chairs almost always have particular owners, their arrangement and degree of comfort displaying the household's hierarchy. If there is only one such chair, it is usually a grossly pampering entity generally known as "Father's chair." Until recently, this was, like the popular image of the eunuch, almost obscenely soft and plump, an enormous behind perched on four tiny legs.

Today, although they bear names like "La-Z-Boy," these chairs have moved with the times. Their Naugahyde skin is stretched tightly over a muscular frame, which is ready to offer a vigorous massage on demand. Still, they continue to cosset with the same practiced abasement of the family dog. Has *it*, after all, ever fetched anyone's slippers or paper other than his master's?

It's worth remembering that sitting down has always been a privilege and a sign of caste. Highborn soldiers served in cavalry units or at least commanded their infantry platoons from horseback. Factory workers stand in front of machines, bank tellers in front of counters, grocery store clerks in front of cash registers—while their supervisors sit at desks.

For centuries, in accounting houses, all but the head clerk wrote and figured standing up at chest-high desks; more recently they were allowed that least comfortable of seats, the stool. The more comfortable the master's chair at home, the more socially traumatic the workplace.

If the easy chair is the antithesis of the work chair, the rocking chair is a subversive attempt to turn the one into the other. The rocker did not, as one might think, evolve from the rocking or hobbyhorse, which is not a chair at all, but a toy. Instead, it grew out of the habit of which most of us were broken in childhood—leaning back on the rear legs of our chair.

Why is this such a pleasure? When you

tilt a chair back to a certain point, the weight of your torso needs no longer be supported by the muscles of the back. The stomach stops sagging forward, which is especially pleasant for those who have just eaten large meals. The body feels weightless, in repose.

However, at just this point, the chair teeters at the verge of falling backwards and requires a certain amount of focused attention to keep from doing so. Those who once smoked cigarettes (or still do) will recognize this combination—the relaxed body, the alert and stimulated mind—as replicating the gift of nicotine, the most social of narcotics.

As with smoking, chair teetering allows an almost inconspicuous flickering of attention from the conversation or work at hand to, depending on your perspective, the maintenance of comfort or avoidance of disaster.

This movement of consciousness, a soothing blend of advance and retreat, can transform socialization into something almost pleasant for the shy and relaxation into something almost bearable for the hyperactive. It is this same oscillation that the rocker makes socially acceptable—at the cost, some would say, of housebreaking it.

Rocking chairs, after all, belong on the front porch or before the fireplace, set out in companionable pairs. Those who teeter are more likely to practice that sport outside a gas station or at a poker party, places where rockers would be seen, at best, as affectations.

Teetering encourages a mischievous alliance between the balancer and the chair—akin to slipping the dog scraps of food under the table. Needless to say, feeding the dog table scraps is considered bad for the dog, just as teetering is considered bad for the chair...as indeed they both may be. However, if chairs could feel, they would, like dogs, delight in such corruption, being for once fellow conspirator instead of slave. ◆

The Stove

~

THE FIRST KITCHEN STOVE in my life was carried up to our second-floor apartment by my grandfather and my mother, who was pregnant with me. The apartment was upstairs over my grandparents' home; they usually rented it to strangers, but my parents were just married, my father had gone off to fight World War II, and my mother wanted just that much distance from her parents: out of sight but not out of reach.

My grandfather never bought anything new when he felt the same thing used would serve as well; his cars were all Cadillacs, all secondhand. So were all his stoves. He had built, and ever after earned his income from, a twenty-four-unit apartment house. To keep it in appliances, he developed intimate contacts with junk dealers near and far. I once drove with him halfway across the state pursuing a

rumor of that rarest of finds, a secondhand, apartment-size gas stove.

The one he found for my mother, a Shaw *Magic Chef* gas range, proved a survivor. A white-enameled, sheet-metal box perched on four long legs, it was already vintage in 1943. But it would be working just fine when I returned, many years later, to live as an adult in the same apartment.

It's a poignant homecoming. Although we had moved out of the place when I was four years old to follow my father to Fort Bliss, Texas, the apartment had made its impression. Images, uncontaminated by words—pure sight, smell, sound—unexpectedly emerge from the deepest recesses of my memory. In these, the kitchen stove exists as a perfectly square block of white: a cube of unadulterated radiant warmth.

I understand this better after I spend the winter there. It is 1978, a year that will be re-membered for a January blizzard that shuts Boston down for a week. The apartment is drafty, poorly insulated, and—by any modern standard—*cold*. Once again, I learn to seek out warmth…and to wait for it, as one does, lying in bed at sunrise, listening to the hiss and bang of hot steam coming slowly up the pipes.

It was just the same in the early 1940s. This is how I came into consciousness: orienting myself to heat. And, because I found it, I grew up into a person who hates the cold but prefers to live in a chilly place—for the pleasure of keeping warm there. My idea of bliss on a freezing morning is to do something time-consuming before a hot stovetop: brew coffee, stir oatmeal, fry eggs.

This may be why I love to cook; it is certainly why I prefer gas to electric stoves. Electric ranges have their advantages—cleanliness, accuracy—but for the seeker of warmth, those virtues are inverted into vices. The electric stove leaves no soot on pots and pans because it has no fire; its heating elements merely glow. A gas oven comes on with a roar; you know it has a fire in its belly. The burners actually burn: there is the flutter of flames, the sibilance and smell of gas…and, that much more, you feel the heat.

However, in the well-insulated, uniformly heated house such surplus heat is obviously unwelcome, and so are the sensual associations it evokes—especially those that cluster around the kitchen stove. We begin to think of them as clinging, even cloying. So vents are installed to whisk them immediately outside.

Where the oven is only another appliance, the microwave is the perfect cooking tool. It projects heat into food without getting hot itself. Because it doesn't use heat to do its work, it makes no sounds of simmering or sizzling, releases no smell of cooking food. Seeing one in a kitchen, you think, not of heat, but of a television, which is to say, of things happening somewhere else.

The situation is very different in this erratically steam-heated, chronically drafty apartment where I am reestablishing my primal bond with the old *Magic Chef*. The kitchen that holds it has been shoehorned into what is really a short hallway, a room so small that I can sit at the table and still reach any pan on the stove.

By the time the meal is ready to be served, moisture from the cooking has condensed on the window glass; heat permeates the room. I eat. The smells, the sounds, the visual emblems of warmth envelop me. I am full and warm and home. ◆

The Mirror

❧

THE MIRROR IS A PRESENCE, NOT A THING. It is the precursor of the telephone, the radio, the television, and other modern inventions that create the illusion of someone…something…being there when nothing is but us. These new devices are more ingenious, but the mirror is far more magical. It has no obvious source of power; it receives no invisible waves of ether; it can never be switched off.

Passive, limpid, the mirror simply reflects and, in doing so, persuades us that it is also somehow *reflective*: that its interiority is deep, even profound. It accomplishes this by reducing the world to two dimensions. The mirror gives us back everything but solidity. Robbed of substance, the world becomes as intangible and ephemeral—and as enigmatic— as a dream.

There are two mirrors in the house: one public, one private. The public one is devoted to reflecting not surface but the absence of surface—space. We hang it in the living or dining room to make those places seem less stuffy and oppressive, to provide an illusion of openness. Pleasingly, if paradoxically, this illusory depth is, unlike real space, edged with intimacy.

We think of windows as the eyes of a house, but a window is only a cavity covered with a piece of glass. Mirrors, like eyes, give access to transmuted space. A wall mirror makes a room at once more personal and more spacious by drawing our eye into a still deeper interior, where the house is dreaming of itself.

The private, bathroom or dresser mirror, on the other hand, is devoted entirely to the reflection of surface…the surface that is us. A window comes closest to a mirror when, looking in or out of one, we encounter someone looking back. In the mirror, we have the relief of knowing that that person is ourself.

Think again. What is most distinctive about our reflection is not the resemblance but the stubbornness. It stares and stares…and so becomes its own person, not like us at all.

Self is a construct created before an audience—first mother, finally the world. In the mirror we find the ultimate beholder—the one who never turns away. Nor, for better or worse, does it ever seem to want to. Our reflection has an obstinate rudeness that we ourselves cannot sustain. It is always we who finally avert our gaze.

This is why it takes such a concerted act of will to look at ourself in a mirror, as opposed to regarding our image looking back at us. Even if we approach a mirror with some simple business of personal care, our eye is caught by our reflected one, which shunts our intent aside.

Mirrors never show us as others see us, because no one else has this stamina to absorb and dominate. If the image in a mirror could be overpowered, we would all be sadists—practice would make us perfect. Instead, it heightens any tendency toward the masochistic. The mirror not only reveals our flaws but does so without blinking. Mirrors, it is said, never lie. Perhaps not, but they force *us* to, all the time.

This is so much so that the term "looking glass" has about it a disingenuous air. A telescope is a glass for looking, without any double entendre. A voyeur may use a telescope, but there is nothing complicit in his actions, nothing that tangles us with him.

In the mirror lie the origins of pornography, because the mirror catches and holds all the erotic ambivalence of the glance. However ignorant of the watcher, the watched on the other side of a one-way mirror is a participant, because to engage in sex before *any* mirror is to accept, court, and seek to arouse the invisible other, the external projection of the self.

The mirror is the eye of the soul (which is why the devil is never reflected in one). Just as we know there is nothing in our head but brain tissue, we also know there is nothing behind the glass of a mirror but a sheet of silvered foil. However, knowing this makes no difference. If the interiority of a mirror is only an illusion, so is the space we feel inside our head.

❧   ❧   ❧

A hot summer night. I've come to a large tree-ringed pool buried deep in a New England woods. At one end of the pool is a concrete dam. Here, where the water is deepest, I stand at the cement edge and look down into a pure reflection of the star-filled sky, total blackness pricked with points of light. I feel a wave of vertigo sweep over me, as if to lose my balance would mean tumbling off the edge of the earth, straight into the heavens.

I teeter there for a moment, savoring the illusion, and then I dive. There is a sudden icy impact as the black sky splits and I plunge into the dark beyond the stars.

The dream of stepping through the looking glass is even older than the looking glass itself and has nothing to do with entering an inverse of the space we already too much inhabit. It is the wish of the dreamer to slip into the dream. Forced always to look out of ourselves at the world, we long for the chance—just once—to be on the outside, looking in. ◆

The Cellar

❧

I AM IN MY FAVORITE ROOM in my grandparents' house. Buried deep in the cellar, it is a tiny place, all but filled with a huge oak desk. When my uncles were young and going to college, my grandfather made it to give them a place to study. He walled it off from the rest of the cellar and then laid a wooden floor over the cold concrete. It is a corner room, with two small casement windows, one set in each of the two massive outside walls made of granite blocks.

Here, besides the desk, is an old-fashioned swivel office chair, a closed wardrobe full of long forgotten naval uniforms, a bookcase sagging under the weight of dusty, mold-covered college texts. The room is cool, even during the hottest days of July.

I'm sixteen, and my parents have allowed me to spend summer vacation working for my grandfather. Every afternoon he takes a long nap, and I come down here to sit, often for hours, sometimes reading, sometimes writing, but always listening. To this room come all the secrets of the house.

Because the cellar has no finished ceiling, the floorboards above my head transmit every step, cough, door closing, or shifting of a chair, as well as every spoken word. I'm not exactly spying—my grandparents say little to each other at any time. My grandmother, bedridden with arthritis, lies in her room in the back of the house listening to the radio in the interludes between visiting nurses. When the radio is switched off, the soft sound of snoring floats down from the other end of the house, where my grandfather is curled up asleep on the living room sofa.

Even so, there is something illicit going on. Both my grandparents know where I am, but descending the cellar stairs I enter a place that cuts them off from my doings and, at the same time, is a sounding board for theirs. Why do I want this?

The attic in my grandparents' house offers one kind of refuge, the cellar another. Only a year or two before, the attic was my favored place. I went there to rise above family things, to soar away. Now, instead, I come down into the cellar to brood.

The word cellar comes from the Latin *cella*, the innermost chamber of a Roman temple, a place of secrets and hidden things. It is next of kin to the word "cell"—a room that by its very location is both close and closed. In the cell, even more than the cellar, time flows thick as syrup, if it moves at all.

In the cellar, unless we come down for some particular purpose, we soon become aware that life is taking place a flight above our head. We all may know that existence goes on without us, but this doesn't make the experience any less unsettling when we unwittingly encounter it doing just that.

Although I don't understand this, what I'm listening to up there is the sound of my own absence. Hidden away in my cellar room, I have a preview of what—if there is a life after death—it might be like to lie, ears pricked, in my coffin. This is no mere fancy, since absence is itself a kind of death…which is why even accidental eavesdropping is an uneasy affair.

The cellar, then, is a different place entirely from the basement, with its linoleum floor, shiny concrete walls, the washing machine and dryer at one end and the workbench at the other, a space for winter playing in the center, scattered with toys.

The basement is a room; the cellar is a place. In days not too far past, when awareness of mortality pressed closer to everyday life, the cellar's purpose was to lift the house up from the earth and into the light—which is to say, to separate the home of the living from the home of the dead. The boundary between them, the cellar became half crypt itself—dark, damp, and smelling of dirt, with swags of cobweb hanging from the walls.

The stairs down to this one are rickety and treacherous. I have slipped and fallen down them more than once. When I was a little boy, a coal-fire furnace burned here all winter, and my grandfather disappeared down them regularly to shovel coal. He reemerged blackened with coal dust, an image that helped shape my imagining of hell.

The coal bin remains, filled with an abandoned phalanx of solid, wood-framed storm windows. As prisoners were sent down into dungeons, so are possessions brought down here—not for safekeeping but to be left to die.

When the house itself is empty, the cellar is cool, quiet, peaceful—a soothing refuge for the fevered adolescent brain. But I never come down *then*. It draws me only when life cheerfully goes about its business overhead and this sanctuary appends to boredom an unexpected thrill—the tremor of the grave yawning beneath my feet. ◆

The Rug

～

As I leave for New York City to move into my first apartment, my grandmother, who cannot give me furniture—I have no way to transport it—presents me instead with a living-room rug.

Unlike the rugs I am familiar with, this one, though slightly shabby, is a silky soft imitation oriental, much too precious to put down on the floor. In the summer I hang it on the wall; in the winter I wrap up in it to sleep. I have blankets, which are more clinging but less reassuring. What the rug brings to sleep is less warmth than weight. As rugs go, it is not all that thick, but, even so, in this regard, no blanket can equal it. I adore it and keep it for decades, until a spate of poor storage ruins it with mildew. I miss it still.

I never call this rug a carpet, although it is as much the one as it is the other. For me, the word "carpet" has something trodden on about it, lovely to look at, perhaps, but not to roll oneself up in for of sheer pleasure. We often speak of a blanket of snow or a carpet of grass, but "rug" resists such usage. The word comes from *rogg*, Old Norse for wool or long hair, and there is something *hairy* in the word's very sound. If no one says a *rug* of grass, no one says a bearskin *carpet*, either. No wonder "rug" became a slang term for a hairpiece, a toupee.

Other mammals are dense with fur; we humans have hair. Fur is thick and soft and smooth; our body hair is sparser, coarser, itchy. We may descend from apes, but in the matter of pelts we are closer kin to sheep. If we had enough body hair to shear, comb, and weave into a blanket, it would, I think, feel very much like wool.

What a mystery we must pose to our pets, slipping in and out of different pelts, some once the proud possession of another animal. The real poser, though, is not why we wrap ourselves in pelts but why we feel the need to have them underfoot. The answer may be as simple as arrogance: showing the rest of the animal kingdom who is hunter and who is quarry. (The word "quarry" itself derives from the Latin for hide or skin.)

Well, maybe so. But we *are* apelike in having feet that are much more like hands than hooves or claws; their bottom surfaces, if not toughened by hard use, remain soft, tender, and highly tactile. Apes, when babies, use their feet to cling tight to their mothers. For them, attachment is literally a fierce toehold on a hank of pelt.

Our poor feet are now too otherwise adapted for such use, and, even if they weren't, would fail to find the sought-for purchase. Even so, somewhere deep inside, they remember. We have too much fun with clothing to feel any nostalgia for the fleece we never had. But—as anyone who has walked barefoot through a shag rug must, if somewhat shamefacedly, admit—we're still groping for our mother's. ◆

The Fire Escape

❧

MY LOWER EAST SIDE apartment is cramped, smelly, and airless. It radiates the aura of years of abuse suffered patiently, of rooms that have long since lost all hope. However, these do face out the back of the building, and looking out of their windows I look down upon a strangely neighborly view: a congested sea of minuscule backyards, some paved with flagstones, some with grass plots and barbecues, some heaped with rubbish, all semishaded by tortured greenery that seems less like trees than weeds run amuck.

There is also a fire escape outside the kitchen window. I decide to use this as a kind of back porch, a place to sit in a beach chair, read, drink wine coolers, and soak in the sun. And so, on the first appropriate sweltering

Sunday, I push back the burglar grate, work the window open, and climb out.

First, I discover that a fire escape is not a porch. A porch is an extension of a house into the open, a room with only one wall. As a boy, when we visited my grandparents, I slept on their front porch. Although it lacked screens and faced a suburban avenue, I felt enclosed in enough privacy to fall into an easy, unthreatened sleep on their plastic-covered chaise lounge.

A fire escape, however, is no part of the house at all; it is something bolted on. To step onto it, you must step out of the house. Your apartment no longer offers protection. Let the window slip and slam shut—what then? A man locked out on his own balcony is a comic figure; a person out on a fire escape, for whatever reason, is a threat. No one will let you in their window; you must get down and find your way back in as best you can.

As it happens, my apartment is on the top floor of the building, but because the door to the roof is always padlocked, I have never been up on top. After a self-conscious half hour perched on a precariously balanced beach chair, I decide to climb up and take a look.

It is hard to find words to explain what I feel there, not because I can't remember but because the sensation seems to belong to the world of dreams. I see the *city* for the first time. It is as if a giant had suddenly picked me up and stood me on his shoulders, so that I could see over the crowd to the parade.

That parade—which is to say, those towering buildings that proclaim, "We are New York"—is very, very far away. I discover that I am lost in an enormous crowd, and, like a child who, having always seen adults from below as a forest of pants legs and shoes, is now lifted up to look into their faces, I feel more seen than seeing, acutely vulnerable. Here on this roof is nothing but pure unmediated cityscape, a sea of barren brick and asphalt, of lumpish heads from which blinks the occasional, unseeing window, the proverbial blind eye.

A frightening place. Of course, the streets below are dangerous, too. Still, I have been out on them at all hours of the day and night. They are a place where you expect danger but also learn to skirt it—and so to ride your fear. But the roof opens up onto an authentic badlands. There is no skirting danger here.

One hot, sleepless summer night, I hear a noise across the way and look out my window to see a Peeping Tom slip down the fire escape and peer into the bedroom windows of the young women who live there. On another night soon after that, I hear—this time directly above my head—the sounds of gunshots and the triumphant cry, "I got him! I got him!" The fire escape is a stairway to an utterly lawless place.

The other stairs, the ones *inside* the building, lead down to one world; these stairs, bolted on the outside of the building, lead up to another. Theoretically, the fire escape also descends to the ground, just as the inner stairs go up to the roof. But, in both instances, the connecting passages are shut. At the top of the inside stairs is a locked door; the bottom tier of the fire escape has been permanently (if illegally) chained at the second floor.

This, of course, was for the sake of "safety," but what it accomplishes instead is to make my own apartment into the connecting passage. Each time my place is broken into, the intruder descends the fire escape, enters through the window (bending up the burglar grate), takes what he wants, and then exits out the front (and only) door, leaving it unlocked behind.

In Boston's North End, where the front stoop serves as a sitting place, the roofs are also claimed as gardens, patios, and arbors. There, in summer at least, the fire escape becomes a communal passageway, lined with open windows and flower boxes.

On the Lower East Side, however, to use these stairs is always to engage in something that, if not exactly furtive, is certainly asocial. Others, braver than myself, regularly climb out of their apartments and ascend the fire escape to the roof, to sunbathe or just hang out. There's no real risk in daytime, they say, and they are right. But the truth is that they are drawn to the badlands sullenness of that starkly unprotected place, and I am not.

I feel a coldness constantly trickling down those stairs. And whenever footsteps approach across the roof, fear's counsel whispers with crazy-making urgency: quickly, quietly, go unlock the door and let them through. ◆

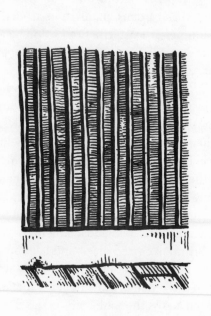

The Mouse

❧

I AM TEACHING AT A PRIVATE SCHOOL. Like many such, it has taken over a large country estate—both grounds and house. Although there is a separate classroom building, dining room, and several dormitories, the main house towers over the campus, a vast, rambling, wood-shingled hulk, with plaster walls and ceilings, fireplaces everywhere, and elaborate wainscoting in every hall and stairway…in other words, mouse heaven.

Here, I have a small apartment cut out of two large bedrooms. One evening late, lying in bed reading, I hear a rustling noise and then a clink. I turn my head to see a mouse departing from my dog's bowl of dry kibble, clutching a chunk of it the size of a hazelnut and heading for the large steam radiator, behind which, apparently, it has a hole.

The strange thing is that my dog—a

large Siberian husky—is lying right beside the bowl. His eyes follow the mouse to its hole and then, a few seconds later, ponder its return, as it strolls right past his nose, climbs into the bowl, helps itself to another piece of kibble, and lugs that, too, back under the radiator.

I don't know why he allows this—sheer laziness, perhaps, or a feeling of good riddance regarding the kibble. This he eats as if it is barely worth the bother of mouthing down, flopped in front of the bowl (he stands up for scraps or canned dog food).

Perhaps it is something else. I've read of foxes living right outside wolf dens, eating scraps of the kill and being generally tolerated. Of course, although dogs kill cats out on the street, they often learn to share quarters amicably with them at home. I think about this the next day, as I get down on my knees and hunt under the radiator until I find the mouse hole and set a mousetrap right in front of it.

It is an interesting fact that a mousetrap does not require bait. Set it alongside a wall, and a mouse will eventually just stumble into it. Today, to convey this message, some mousetrap makers form the trip lever to look like a slice of Swiss. The notion that the dab of peanut butter, the sliver of cheese, is necessary is a sop to our conscience. It allows us to blame the mouse for its own death. It also transforms an ugly necessity into a little moral drama. In the mousetrap lie the origins of the tale.

I don't think I've ever felt any fondness for house mice (field mice, with their light brown coats and soft white bellies, are a different matter, although I trap them, too). But I sometimes do feel neighborly toward them, a strange balance of irritation and acceptance, reflected, perhaps, in the fact that only a single letter separates pet from pest.

The problem, of course, is not mouse but mice. *En masse*, they are relentless, their habits disgusting, their nests, when uncovered, irredeemably verminous. The individual mouse, the mouse as metaphor, is another matter. Tiny, shabbily gray, unthreateningly timid, the quintessential homebody, the mouse gives legitimacy to our private space by transforming it into an entire universe. However humble our habitation, the presence of the mouse expands it into something dangerous, awe-inspiring, and huge—the castle where we play king.

The poorer the house, the more appreciated the illusion. The ability of the mouse to feed on crumbs can make the crust seem like a feast. Consequently, it is over the imagination of the poor that the mouse has the strongest hold, at once threatening and enhancing the little that they have.

On the other hand, the mouse's home, the place beyond the mouse hole, is not just another living space, a separate apartment, but the house within the house, home squared. From this perspective, the mouse hole is the doorway into a kingdom of intimate space, the place we also perceive through the window of a doll's house.

This is exactly how the illustrators of children's books depict it, with the resident asleep in an easy chair pulled up to a tiny fire, comfortable, warm, safe, two realms away from the dark predators that stalk the night.

What this picture does not show is that, in its dreams, the mouse becomes a rat. The rat is the mouse blown up beyond cuteness. Although equally timid, its size makes its skulky nervousness seem psychotic, as it makes the long, pink, naked tail reptilian and repulsive.

Even after you have seen one, it is hard to admit how *large* rats are. Years later, a friend's dog catches two late at night in the kitchen of my tiny Maine cottage, one after the other—each the size of a gray squirrel. I am angry at the dog; I don't want to know that such things are in my house, slipping out of the walls at night to roam about at will.

What disturbs me most about the rat, however, is not its size but its ability to go almost anywhere a mouse can (its skull is jointed so that it can squeeze through the tiniest cracks). This reverses and unsettles the deep belief that I am somehow safest when buried deepest in my nest. It is not the burglar but the rat—king of misrule in the house as nightmare—who lurks beneath the bed. Before the presence of the rat, intimacy means not being able to escape.

Hence the cat, who is in every way the antithesis of rodent. Mysterious, but also meticulous, sleek, bold, and quick, it resolves the contradictions posed by the mouse or rat by killing it. The cat represents the triumph of the forces of order over the forces of disorder, forces which in ourselves are in confused, perpetual battle. The cat is the avatar of that cool gnostic deity *control*: equal parts good and evil—a dangerous thing to worship, but a necessary household god. ◆

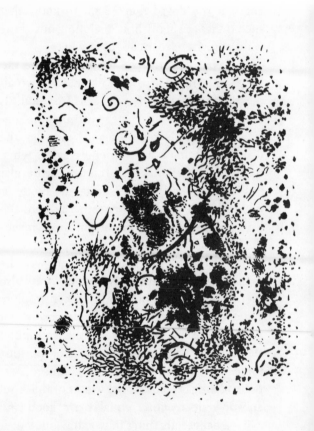

Epilogue

Dust

❧

All are of the dust, and all turn to dust
again.

—*Eccles. 3:20*

I'M LIVING ALONE, between female com-
panions, in a small one-bedroom apartment. My tiny living room—at once
office, entertainment center, and library—is
jammed with furniture, electronic equipment,
books, papers, more books, more papers. My
work table, which takes up one wall, is so
heaped with the detritus of my trade that I
have to put my coffee cup on an old ashtray
stand beside my chair.

Because this is a work table, however,
the things on it are in perpetual—if extremely

intermittent—motion. Files are eventually shifted, books opened and closed, mail at last read and tossed aside, magazines riffled through. There is no surface still quite long enough for dust to gather there, and so I act as if there were none at all.

Wrong. Dust, like madness, blindness, moral decay, doesn't appear out of the blue with the sudden violence of a summer storm. It drifts down softly, an incessant, imperceptible sift. It gathers incrementally on the understruts of chairs, on top of every book on every shelf of every bookcase. It spreads itself in a grey film across every sash bar on every window. It coats the tops of cabinets, clings to every fiber in the several scatter rugs, coheres into dust kittens under the radiators.

Still I don't see it. I come in from the kitchen in the morning, turn on the radio, and sit down to work, unaware that anything is different…although, by now, it is very, very different. How can I stare for hours every day at the large framed picture hanging across from where I work and not notice that its glass face has—for several weeks—been smutted over with a greasy haze?

There are various answers to this question, I know, but surely one of them is that, unless it is disciplined to do otherwise, in such situations consciousness withdraws. And who can fail to sympathize? If premonition, that aura felt before the arrival of bad news, could be given substance, it would be this silent plague.

Dirt is what we track into the house ourselves; dust comes of its own accord. If there were no dust, housekeeping would be an art form, not a chore, and men would do it gladly. Dust, like inflation, takes the joy out of industry by relentlessly diminishing its rewards. Something carefully cleaned should stay clean until used—until, that is, we have the pleasure of dirtying it ourselves.

Instead, dust mocks the work ethic. If it came as a perpetual rain of dirt, we would learn to cope. But it never piles up in inches in deserted places; its signature is the smudge. Dust comes from everywhere—and from nowhere. The black soot that appears fresh daily on the living room windowsill—where does it come from? What *is* it? Dust is ants without ant traps; a drip from the ceiling that will not cease and can't be fixed; a dead rodent eternally rotting in the wall—existence in the act of soiling itself.

Housecleaners are born, not made. They move through life, dustcloth in hand, leaving behind the brilliant, polished surfaces that the rest of us, for whom a sense of balance comes with stasis, wrongly believe to be the norm. They know, as we do not, that life is work and that rest is not an end but only the briefest of intermissions.

Even so, we others at least cherish the clarity that comes with cleaning up. Usually it is the prospect of a visit—or, even worse, an unexpected knocking at the door—that brings us to. The filth falls into focus. The vacuum cleaner is dragged out of the closet; the dustcloth and the gaggle of cleaning sprays pulled from under the kitchen sink. The wet mop is plied across the floor, and one bucket after another of astonishingly dirty water slops into the toilet's maw.

The aftermath of all this flurry is surely one of life's most delicious calms. We sink into a chair and look around. All the colors are brightened, the air is fresh and sweet, the light flows unimpeded through utterly transparent space. The outside sparkles through the spotless window glass; the inside has an intimate burnished sheen.

This one brief but brilliant moment—and how we yearn for it to last—is as close as some of us will ever come to sanity, to knowing what it might be like to have, for once and forever, the murk all swept aside. ◆

Copyright

Acknowledgments

❧

❧

It's the other houses, strange staircases, odd smells, unfamiliar furniture and topography that the proverbial old dogs dream about in their senility and decrepitude, not new masters. And the trick is not to disturb them.

—Joseph Brodsky,
Watermark

❧

Other Books by John Thorne

Simple Cooking
Outlaw Cook
Serious Pig

About the Author

John Thorne, the author of *Outlaw Cook*, is an essayist and food writer who edits and publishes the culinary newsletter *Simple Cooking*. An "army brat" who spent his childhood traveling around the world, Thorne now savors life as a homebody in Steuben, Maine.